**Symbols of Freedom**

## National Parks

# Hawaii Volcanoes National Park

M.C. Hall

Heinemann Library
Chicago, Illinois

Customer Service  888-454-2279
Visit our website at www.heinemannlibrary.com

Page layout by Richard Parker and Maverick Design
Photo research by Maria Joannou
Illustrations by Jeff Edwards
Printed and bound in China by South China Printing Company Limited

10 09 08 07 06
10 9 8 7 6 5 4 3 2 1

**Library of Congress Cataloging-in-Publication Data**
Hall, Margaret, 1947-
   Hawaii Volcanoes National Park / Margaret Hall.
      p. cm. --  (National parks)
Includes bibliographical references and index.
ISBN 1-4034-6700-5 (library binding-hardcover) -- ISBN 1-4034-6707-2 (pbk.)
1.  Hawaii Volcanoes National Park--Juvenile literature. 2.  Volcanoes--Hawaii--Juvenile literature.
I. Title.  II. Series.
   DU628.H33H35 2005
   919.69'1--dc22

                              2004030389


**Acknowledgments**
The author and publishers are grateful to the following for permission to reproduce copyright material:
Corbis pp. **9**, **14** (Buddy Mays), **22** (David Muench), **20** (Douglas Peebles), **13** (Jim Sugar), **15** (Michael S. Yamashita), **10** (Michael T. Sedam), **25** (Michael T. Sedam), **21** (Robert Holmes), **19** (Roger Ressmeyer), **17** (Ted Streshinsky); Getty Images/The Image Bank p. **16** (Art Wolfe); Getty Images/ Photodisc pp. **29**, **30**, **31**, **32**; Library of Congress p.**8**; National Park Service p. **18**; NGDC p. **12**; OzImages p. **11** (Cyd Read); Photo Resource Hawaii/ David Schrichtem pp. **4**, **24**; Photo Resource Hawaii pp. **5**, **27** (G. Brad Lewis), **26** (Marc Schechter); Topham Picturepoint/ The ImageWorks  p. **23** (Sonda Dawes); Topham Picturepoint/ImageWorks p. **7** (Joe Carini)

Cover photograph of Kilauea erupting reproduced with permission of Corbis (Douglas Peebles)

Some words are shown in bold, **like this**. You can find out what they mean by looking in the glossary.

# Contents

# Our National Parks

**National parks** are areas of land set aside for people to visit and enjoy **nature**. These parks do not belong to one person. They belong to everyone in the United States.

Kilauea is the world's most **active volcano**.

There are more than 50 national parks in the United States. Hawaii Volcanoes National Park is one of the country's most unusual parks.

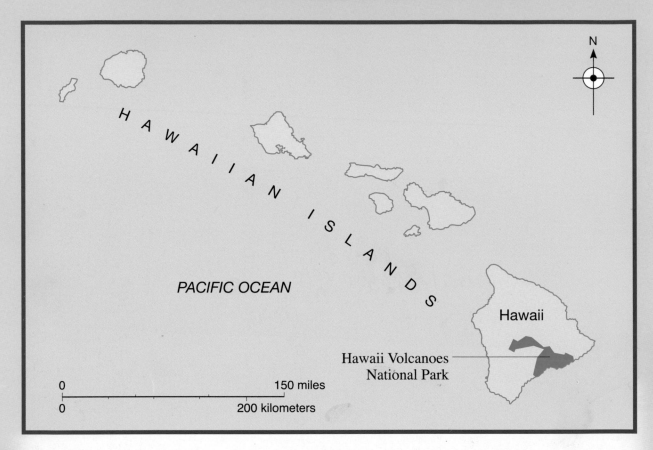

N

H A W A I I A N   I S L A N D S

PACIFIC OCEAN

Hawaii

Hawaii Volcanoes National Park

0                    150 miles

0                    200 kilometers

Hawaii Volcanoes National Park is on the island of Hawaii. This island is the biggest of the many islands that are part of the state of Hawaii. It is sometimes called the Big Island.

The Hawaiian Islands were made by **volcanoes**. Some of these volcanoes are still **erupting**. The park is named for these volcanoes.

# Hawaii Long Ago

Honolulu harbor in Hawaii
was a busy port by 1910.

The first people to live in Hawaii came from
other islands in the Pacific Ocean about
1,600 years ago. In the 1800s, people from
other countries traveled to Hawaii to trade
for things that grew there.

Scientists came to Hawaii to study the volcanoes.

Scientists also came to the island of Hawaii to study **volcanoes**. In 1916 the United States **government** made the area a **national park**.

# Visiting Hawaii Volcanoes National Park

Hawaii is far from the rest of the United States. Most visitors fly there to visit Hawaii Volcanoes National Park. They come to see the **volcanoes** and the **wildlife**.

Most of Hawaii never has cold weather.
Visitors come to the park all year long.
They camp, hike, and learn about volcanoes.

# Mauna Loa and Kilauea

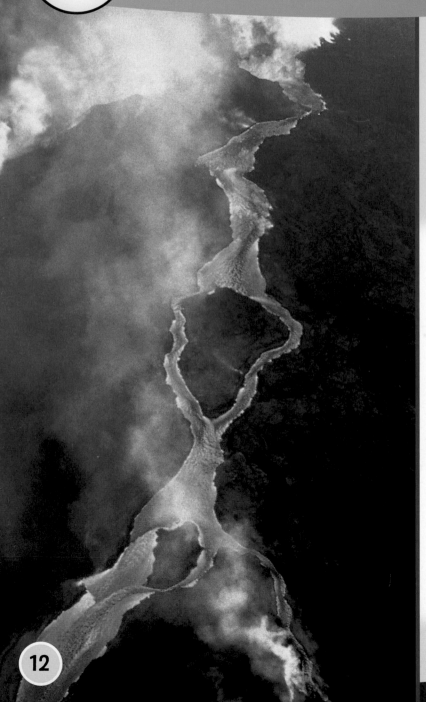

Mauna Loa is the largest **volcano** in the world. This volcano has **erupted** thirteen times in the last 100 years. The last **eruption** was in 1984.

Kilauea is the world's most **active volcano**. It has erupted more than 40 times in the last 100 years. The last eruption started in 1983 and is still going on.

# Exploring Kilauea

People can hike around the edge of Kilauea. Sometimes they can even go inside an old part of the **volcano**.

People can only walk on old, cooled lava.

gas

**Lava**, **steam**, or gas comes from the volcano during an **eruption**. Visitors must watch from a safe place.

# Looking at Lava

During an **eruption**, **lava** is hot enough to burn anything it touches. As it flows, the lava cools off. Its color changes from red to orange to black. After a long time, it becomes hard rock.

Visitors can see lava from old eruptions. Cooled lava can be rough or smooth. Some cooled lava looks like ribbons of rock.

# Lava Meets the Sea

Parts of the park are near the water. Visitors go there to watch **lava** pour into the sea. **Steam** forms when hot lava hits the cold water.

The lava breaks up into tiny pieces in the water. When the pieces cool, they form black sand. Visitors come to see the unusual sand.

# Other Sights

Visitors can explore the Thurston Lava Tube. A lava tube is a tunnel formed by **lava**. It is dark and wet inside.

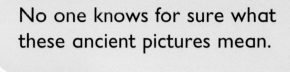
No one knows for sure what these ancient pictures mean.

People also come to see pictures made by the first Hawaiians. The pictures were carved into rock more than 1,000 years ago.

# Park Plants

Some parts of the park get a lot of rain. Many trees, flowers, and vines grow there. Some of these plants only grow in Hawaii.

The koa tree only grows in Hawaii.

Hot **lava** kills trees and plants. After the lava cools, new plants start to grow. Sometimes the plants grow out of cracks in the lava.

# Park Animals

Green sea turtles come to rest on the black sand beach.

Visitors sometimes see humpback whales in the ocean near the park. Small animals like birds, bats, turtles, and rabbits live inside the park.

Visitors are asked not to feed the birds in the park.

The most interesting park bird is the nene. It is only found in Hawaii. These birds do not do much flying. They walk on cool, hard **lava** rock.

# Park People

**Park rangers** help visitors learn about Hawaii Volcanoes National Park. Rangers lead hikes and give talks about **volcanoes** and **wildlife**.

The hula is a traditional dance in Hawaii.

Every year there is a Hawaiian **festival** at the park. Visitors learn about **traditional** Hawaiian music and dances. They eat traditional foods like **poi**.

# Map of Hawaii Volcanoes National Park

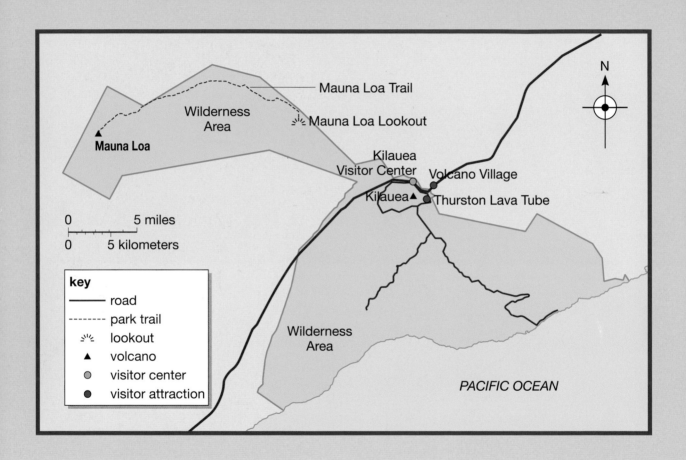

N

Mauna Loa Trail

Wilderness
Area

Mauna Loa Lookout

▲
**Mauna Loa**

Kilauea
Visitor Center

Volcano Village

Kilauea ▲

Thurston Lava Tube

| 0 | 5 miles |
| 0 | 5 kilometers |

**key**

| | |
|---|---|
| —— | road |
| ------ | park trail |
| ᗜ | lookout |
| ▲ | volcano |
| ● | visitor center |
| ● | visitor attraction |

Wilderness
Area

*PACIFIC OCEAN*

# Timeline

| | |
|---|---|
| *1,600 years ago* | First people settle in Hawaii |
| *1823* | First non-Hawaiian visitors see Kilauea |
| *1912* | U.S. **government** sets up the Hawaiian Volcano Observatory to study the **volcanoes** |
| *1913* | Thurston Lava Tube is discovered |
| *1916* | U.S. government sets land aside as Hawaii Volcanoes National Park |
| *1959* | Hawaii becomes the 50th state |
| *1960* | **Lava** from Kilauea destroys homes and villages |
| *1983* | Kilauea's latest **eruption**. The eruption is still going on. |
| *1984* | Mauna Loa's latest eruption. The volcano has not **erupted** again. |
| *1986–1990* | Lava from Kilauea destroys homes in Kalapana |

# Glossary

**active volcano** volcano that is erupting

**erupt** to send out lava, gas, or steam

**eruption** time when a volcano is sending out lava, gas, or steam

**festival** celebration

**government** group of people that makes laws for and runs a country

**lava** melted rock from the center of the earth

**national park** natural area set aside by the government for people to visit

**nature** the outdoors and the wild plants and animals found there

**park ranger** man or woman who works in a national park and shares information about the wildlife and unusual sights of the park

**poi** pastelike food made by pounding the root of a Hawaiian plant

**steam** tiny droplets of water that can be seen in the air

**traditional** something done in the way it was done in the past

**volcano** hill or mountain formed by melted rock and ash from inside the earth

**wildlife** wild animals of an area

# Find Out More

## Books

An older reader can help you with these books:

Furgang, Kathy. *Kilauea: Hawaii's Most Active Volcano.* New York, N.Y.: PowerKids Press, 2001.

McAuliffe, Emily. *Hawaii: Facts and Symbols.* Mankato, Minn.: Capstone, 2000.

Nelson, Sharlene. *Hawaii Volcanoes National Park.* Minneapolis, Minn.: Sagebrush Bound, 2001.

Simon, Seymour. *Danger! Volcanoes.* Oklahoma City, Okla.: Seastar Publishing Company, 2002.

Wood, Lily. *Volcanoes.* New York, N.Y.: Scholastic, 2001.

## Address

To find out more about Hawaii Volcanoes National Park, write to:

Hawaii Volcanoes National Park
P.O. Box 52
Hawaii National Park, HI 96718-0052

# Index